EYEWITNESS
EXPLORERS

Seashore

Written by
DAVID BURNIE

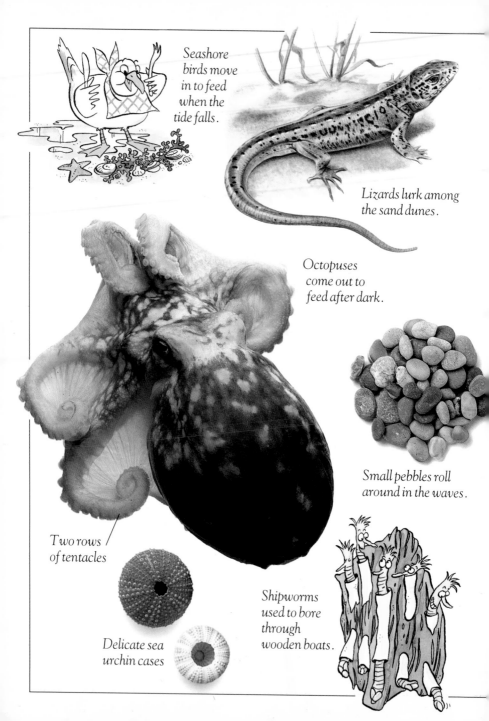

Seashore birds move in to feed when the tide falls.

Lizards lurk among the sand dunes.

Octopuses come out to feed after dark.

Small pebbles roll around in the waves.

Two rows of tentacles

Delicate sea urchin cases

Shipworms used to bore through wooden boats.

EYEWITNESS

EXPLORERS

Seashore

Written by
DAVID BURNIE

DK PUBLISHING, INC.
www.dk.com

LONDON, NEW YORK, MUNICH,
MELBOURNE and DELHI

Editor Claire Bampton
Art editor Rebecca Johns
Project editor Mary Ling
Production Catherine Semark
Editorial consultant Kathie Way
U.S. Editor Jill Hamilton

First Paperback Edition, 1997
8 10 9 7
Published in the United States by
DK Publishing, Inc., 375 Hudson Street
New York, New York 10014

See our complete product line at
www.dk.com

A CIP catalog record is available from the Library of Congress.
ISBN 0-7894-1681-6

Color reproduction by Colorscan, Singapore
Printed and bound in Spain by Artes Gráficas Toledo S.A.U.
D.L. TO: 1224 – 2003

Contents

The seashore

Everyone likes the seaside. In warm weather it is a good place to keep cool and there is always lots to do and see. In this book you can find out about seashore wildlife and discover what makes one piece of coastline very different from another.

Hidden away

Part of being a seashore explorer is knowing where to look for animals. The spiny squat lobster hides under stones when the tide is out.

Always put animals back where you found them!

Exploring the shore

You can find out a lot about seashore wildlife without any equipment at all. But you will discover even more if you have a dip net and keep a notebook to record what you have found.

Dip net

On the alert

Some seashore animals are stuck to rocks, so they cannot run away. This makes them easy to investigate (study). Other animals are always on the alert for danger and will run or swim away if they see you coming.

A crab is always alert.

For many plants and animals the seashore is a year-round home.

Keeping a notebook
A notebook helps you remember what you have seen on the shore. Drawing something is a good way of finding out exactly how it is shaped. You don't have to be a wildlife artist to keep a notebook, but with practice you might turn into one!

Remember to record exactly where and at what time of year the seashore creature was found.

What shapes the shore?

The shore is always on the move. In some places the sea eats away at the land, so the shore moves back. In other places it builds up banks of sand or gravel, so the shore moves forward to the sea. By knowing what to look for and how the sea affects the shore, you can see these changes at work.

First waves
When waves smash against a cliff, water is forced through cracks in the rock.

Natural arch formed by waves

Second stage
In time, the rock breaks apart. Sometimes, it leaves a hole which widens to form an arch.

Final fall down
The rock arch gets wider and wider, until one day it collapses into the sea. All that is left is a tall rocky stump, called a stack.

Stack

Graded grains

When the sea attacks a rocky shore, it breaks up the rock and then pushes the pieces along the coast. It can move heavy boulders only a short distance, but it can carry sand a long way. The pebbles shown here were collected at regular intervals along a 12-mile-long coastline.

Rocks are broken off by the pounding of waves.

Large pebbles break up to make smaller ones.

Coarse pebbles are small enough to roll around in the waves.

The motion of the waves wears the pebbles away to gravel.

Making a shore profile

If you draw part of a shoreline, you can see where the shore is changing. Cliffs and rocky stacks show where the shore is being eaten away. Level gravel and mud often show that the shore is building up.

The pebbles eventually break up to make sand.

Making waves

Waves are made by the wind. When the wind blows over the ocean, it pushes and drags against the surface. The surface starts to ripple and waves form. Waves can travel huge distances. A storm can whip up waves in one part of an ocean, but many hours may pass before they reach the shore.

Nearly three-quarters of the Earth is covered by water.

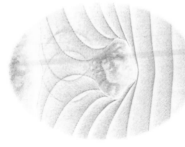

Here you can see how waves change direction as they pass an island. Behind the island the waves meet head-on.

Waves on the turn

Waves normally travel in straight lines. But if one end of a wave enters shallow water, it slows down. The rest of the wave keeps moving as before, so the whole wave turns.

How waves work

If you watch a wave, the water seems to move forward. But if you float something on the water, you will find that it stays in more or less the same place. Each time a wave passes, the water actually moves in circles.

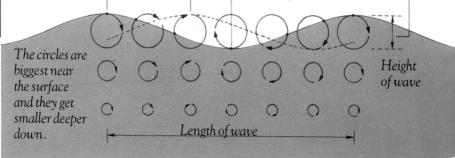

The circles are biggest near the surface and they get smaller deeper down.

Height of wave

Length of wave

Making a paper boat
To make your own paper boat you will need a square piece of paper.

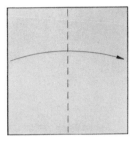 

1 Fold the piece of paper in half.

2 Fold the paper in half again from top to bottom.

3 Fold the top sheet of paper backward to form a triangle.

 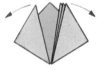

4 Fold the other three quarters of paper in the opposite direction.

5 Pull open the triangle into a cup and fold it together to form a square.

6 Gently pull out on the two halves to get your boat ready to sail.

How waves break
When waves approach the shore, they get taller and closer together. The bottom of each wave drags against the seabed and slows down, but the top of the wave keeps moving. Eventually, the surface topples over and crashes onto the beach.

Tides and zones

The world's highest tides are found in the Bay of Fundy, between Canada and the United States. In six hours, the sea level can rise or fall by the height of a four-story building. But even small tides have an important effect on the shore's wildlife.

When the Sun and Moon are in a line with the Earth, tides are extra high.

What causes tides?

Gravity causes tides. The sea is held in place by the Earth's gravity. The gravity of the Sun and Moon tugs at the Earth's seawater and pulls it toward them.

Zones on the shore

Some seashore animals and plants need to be in water all the time. Others can survive for a while in air when the tide is out. These differences mean that seashore wildlife is arranged in zones, like the layers of a sandwich.

Top shells live on the middle or lower shore.

Oarweed grows in or below the lower shore.

Starfish usually live below the level of the lowest tide.

Most shore crabs can live in and out of water.

subtidal zone

lower shore

Time for a meal
When the tide falls, many shorebirds come to the water's edge looking for small animals stranded as the water level drops.

Making a profile
On some shores, the zones are easy to see. You can keep a record of them by making a shore profile showing what kinds of plants and animals live at different levels. See if you can spot the very highest barnacle on a rocky shore.

Sketch in the animals and plants, showing where they live on the shore.

Mussels close up at low tide, to keep from drying out.

Periwinkles wander high into the splash zone.

Water pipits feed all over the shore above water.

Oystercatchers use their long bills to dislodge limpets.

Sea lettuce grows in pools in the middle and upper shore.

Sea roach

Shrimps will die out of water.

Limpets can survive in air for a long time.

| middle shore | upper shore | splash zone |

Signs in the sand

A sandy or muddy shore is a perfect place for finding tracks. When the tide falls it leaves a smooth, damp surface. Animal feet sink in as they walk over the sand or mud, leaving a telltale trail of tracks.

A gull's middle toe is straight, but its other toes are curved.

A gull walks with its feet turned slightly inward

Deep claw marks

Gull tracks
A gull has three forward-pointing toes. These toes are connected by flaps of skin called webs, which help the gull to swim.

Going for a run
Dog's paws have four small pads near the front, and a larger pad at the back. If the dog is running, its claws leave deep marks in the sand.

Webbed toes for swimming

Feet on the beach
The depth of your footprints and the distance between them depend on how fast you are moving. When you look at footprints on the beach, see if you can work out whether the person that left them was walking or running.

When someone is walking, they leave an even footprint.

Four-toed tracks

Cormorants usually live on rocks, but
sometimes they leave tracks on sandy or
muddy beaches. A cormorant
foot has four outward-pointing
toes, joined by a web of skin.
All its toes are straight, and
the front toe is the longest.
Cormorants have short legs,
so their tracks are close together.

*Herons have a long
stride, so their tracks
are often wide apart.*

Webbed toes

*Cormorants are
not very good at
walking, so they do
not leave long trails.*

Heron tracks

Herons have three forward-
pointing toes and one toe that
points backward. Herons hunt
by wading into the water,
and they often leave tracks
on muddy sand.

*A human footprint is narrowest in
the middle, where the foot arches.*

*Backward-
pointing toe*

*When someone is running,
their toes leave more of a
mark than their heels.*

Clean away

When the tide returns, the sea wipes
the tracks away, just like someone
erasing a blackboard.

Beach detective

Every day, the sea throws all kinds of objects onto the shore. These include shells, seaweed, and even old coins. For a beach detective, the best place to start investigating is the strandline – the line of "leftovers" washed up by the tide.

Dead shells lose their color.

High rollers
These strange objects are underwater plant fibers rolled into balls by the waves.

Hidden danger
The animals that live in these cone shells have poisonous stings! Take care.

Fibers tangled to make a ball

Driftwood often looks like bones, or even animals.

Sea smooth
Pieces of wood are worn smooth by the sea.

Stranded starfish
If a starfish is washed up on the beach, it will dry out and die. Its dry body then takes a long time to break down.

A dried-out starfish is stiff.

Live starfish have flexible arms.

Long, flattened beak

Weed out of water
After storms, seaweed is dislodged and thrown high up on the beach. This bladder wrack has dried and become stiff.

Coral treasure
In warm parts of the world, you may find pieces of colorful coral.

Piece of glass

The sea keeps beach sand on the move and grinds up shells and stones.

Shell fragment

No spines
Sea urchin shells are very fragile (weak) and they quickly get broken up by waves.

Urchins are covered with spines when they are alive.

Cone shell with short, pointed spire

Cockle shells in two halves

Making a mess
Not everything on the beach is natural. Plastic does not decay in the sea and plastic bottles and bags can float across the oceans.

Beach bones
Skulls are good for detective work, because they show how an animal lived. This skull belonged to a brown pelican that fished with its huge beak.

19

High and dry

For humans, a cliff can be a dangerous place, so it's important to be careful when you go on a clifftop walk. But for some seashore animals, cliffs are places of safety. Seabirds breed on cliffs because their enemies cannot reach them there. For a few weeks every year, some sea cliffs are home to many noisy birds, jammed tightly together on every rocky ledge.

Mother bee arriving with food

Free flight
Gulls use the breeze that blows up over cliffs to lift themselves up, so they can stay in the air without flapping their wings. By adjusting the slant of its wings, a gull can hover and look for food.

Miniature mine
A sandy, sheltered slope makes a perfect nest site for a mining bee. The female bee digs out a branching tunnel. She stocks each side branch with some pollen and lays an egg in each.

Birdwatcher's paradise
Cliffs are wonderful places for birdwatching, particularly if you have a pair of binoculars. In spring and early summer, lots of nesting birds lay their eggs on different parts of the cliffs. In autumn and winter, many seabirds leave the cliffs for the open sea.

Clowns of the clifftops

It's easy to recognize a puffin because it has a striped beak and bright orange feet. Puffins nest in burrows, which they dig in clifftop sod. They often stand at the entrance to their burrows, cleaning their feathers and trying to flap their stubby wings.

Noisy neighbors

Kittiwakes nest on high rocky ledges. They make their nests from seaweed glued together with droppings. Kittiwakes often nest in huge numbers, and their shrieking calls fill the air.

Life on a ledge

Murres do not make nests. Each female lays a single egg on a rocky ledge, and stands guard over it. One end of her egg is very pointed, so that the egg can only roll around in a circle. This makes it less likely to fall over the edge.

Ground floor

Cormorants nest at the bottom of the cliffs, just above the waves. They lay three or four eggs in a seaweed nest. Cormorants often stand with their wings open, drying their feathers in the breeze.

Just visiting

In many parts of the world, the seashore is visited by different animals at different times of the year. In winter, many birds arrive on the coast from colder places far away. In spring and summer, the shore is a place where animals raise their young. Summer also sees quite different visitors to the shore, when humans flock to the coast for their vacations.

Pink-footed geese migrating along the coast

Homing in
The coast is a good winter home for birds, since it is usually warmer than places farther inland.

Summer visitors
During the summer, the seashore wildlife may be harmed because in some places there are too many hotels and cars, and too much litter.

When you visit the beach, always wear sunscreen to protect your skin from the sun's harmful rays.

When you go home, leave nothing behind but your footprints!

Thief in the night

In warm parts of the world, the mongoose visits the shore after dark. It eats crabs and other seashore animals, and it also sniffs out turtle eggs buried in the sand. When it finds a turtle's nest, it digs up the eggs and feasts on them.

A seal pup may remain on shore for three months, before entering the sea.

Coming ashore to breed

Seals spend a lot of their time in the water, but they give birth on land. Seals do not like to be close to humans. They come ashore on distant parts of the coast, where they can raise their young without being disturbed.

Dolphins are often friendly to humans.

Joining in

Dolphins are very clever animals that are full of curiosity. They often swim just in front of boats and enjoy playing with humans. In some parts of the world, dolphins come close to the shore to be near swimmers.

Fish out of water

The California grunion is a fish that lays its eggs on land. Grunion gather close to the shore after dark and then wriggle onto the beach to lay their eggs. As soon as the grunion have finished, they return to the sea.

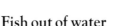

Shell shapes

When you walk along the shore, you will find lots of empty shells. A shell is a special kind of shelter. It protects an animal from its enemies, and keeps it from drying out at low tide.

Separated
Many shells have two halves that hinge together. After the owner dies, the two halves may soon become separated.

Empty periwinkle shells are often used as homes by hermit crabs.

Cowries
A cowrie shell has a slit-shaped opening lined with ridgelike teeth.

Olive shells
These shells look a bit like cones but they are longer and thinner. This shell has an orange opening.

Wrap-around shell
A cone shell has an almost flat spiral at one end. The older the shell, the more turns its spiral has.

Corkscrew shells
Many shells have a long spiral at one end, like a corkscrew.

Remains of the hinge that once joined shell to its opposite half

The top of the tightly coiled spire is the oldest part of this shell.

Smooth lining
Shells are often rough or bumpy on the outside, but inside they are usually very smooth.

Smooth, shiny layer on inside of shell

Taken for a ride

The outside of a shell is often turned into a home by other animals and plants. Barnacles need a solid surface to live on and a shell suits them very well.

The barnacles get a better chance of finding food if the shell's owner moves about.

It is worth sifting and sorting pebbles and gravel to find small shells like these for your collection.

Seashells to keep

Shells like this scallop are fun to collect and keep. Collecting empty shells does not harm wildlife, unlike buying shells in shops.

A barnacle is really a body case made of separate plates.

Going to pieces

After a sea animal dies, its shell is slowly worn away. Eventually, all that is left are tiny pieces.

This conch shell had knobs on it which have been worn away by the sea.

This brown fig cone comes from the Indian and Pacific Oceans.

High rise

Slipper shells grow in piles, with several shells stacked up on top of each other.

Borers and burrowers

It's easy to dig a hole in the sand, but imagine being able to dig one through solid rock! Many seashore animals protect themselves by digging. Some live in rocks or wood, and others live in sand or mud.

Piddock shell in rock

Shell halves have rough edges.

Burrowing in the sand

Tusk shells are mollusks that spend their lives in deep water, partly buried in sand. Their shells are often washed up on beaches. A tusk shell collects food from the sand with its short tentacles.

Boring through rock

The two halves of the piddock shell work just like a drill bit, turning one way and then the other, boring through soft rock.

Scooping out a home

Sea urchins use their spines and mouthparts to scrape a hollow shelter in solid rock. The spines are made of a mineral called calcite, which is similar to our teeth.

Sea urchins shelter in rock.

Hiding below the surface

Look carefully when you are walking at low tide for signs of worms below the surface. The sticky feeding tubes of the sand mason are easy to spot.

Sand mason

Water, sand, and mud enter through one end of the burrow.

Waste piles up here

Tubes of sand and small shells

Mud, lovely mud

Mud and sand are perfect hiding places for animals with soft bodies. A lugworm lives in a U-shaped burrow. It swallows sand and mud that falls into the burrow's entrance, digesting any food that it contains. The lugworm then squirts waste sand and mud out of the other end of the burrow, like someone squeezing toothpaste from a tube!

Tube may be up to 10 inches long.

Head

13 pairs of red feathery gills

Lugworm's tail

Sinking the ship

Shipworms are not really worms at all, but mollusks, similar to piddocks. Shipworms use their shells to bore through wood, digesting wood flakes as they move along. When all boats were made of wood, shipworms were a serious pest.

Seashore fish

Many seashore animals stay in one place, so it is easy to get a close look at them. Watching fish is a bit more tricky. Fish are always on the alert and they will usually swim for cover if they see you coming.

Keeping upright

The seahorse is an unusual small fish that swims upright. Its body is covered with bony plates and it uses its tail to anchor itself to underwater plants. If you look at its head, you can see how it gets its name.

Finger-sized fish

Gobies are small fish that nearly always live in shallow water. They have large eyes and are quick to spot any sign of danger. This is a black goby, which is common on rocky coasts.

Some gobies have suckers to fasten themselves to rocks.

Paddle-shaped tail fin helps goby to swim.

The tompot blenny has a long fin along the top of its body.

Fast mover

Blennies live in tide pools in many parts of the world. If you try to scoop one up with a net, you will find that it can change direction with lightning speed.

The butterfly blenny lives both near the shore and in deep water.

Swimming like a fish

If someone is a good swimmer people often say that they "swim like a fish." But fish don't swim like humans. Most of them push from side to side with their tail fins and use their other fins to steer. If you have some flippers, you can try this for yourself.

1 Hold your arms down by your sides. Wearing the flippers, kick with your feet.

2 As you move forward, keep your arms at your side and your head up above the water.

Swimming like a fish is quite hard work, so only try it in shallow water.

The male cuckoo wrasse has blue markings on a yellow background.

A splash of color

Many fish have dull colors, so they can hide easily. But instead of being drab, wrasses that live in deep water are often brilliantly colored. These two fish are cuckoo wrasses. The male and female look quite different.

The female cuckoo wrasse is mainly orange. Young male fish are orange too.

Look carefully

Life is not easy for seashore animals.
They have to find enough to eat, but they
also have to make sure that they do not get
eaten themselves. Many escape their enemies
by having special shapes and colors
so that they match their background.

Find that fish!
A pipefish has a very long body and is not
much thicker than a pencil. It hides
among underwater plants and
sucks in pieces of floating
food through its mouth.

Disappearing crab
The long-legged
spider crab hides
in seaweed and it even
fastens small pieces to its body.
Can you spot its claws and its
long spidery legs?

*Straight-
nosed
pipefish*

A perfect match
On the seabed there is nothing to hide behind.
Flatfish and rays settle on the
sand or gravel and use their
special markings to
blend in with their
background.

*This ray has brown
and white markings
that look like the sunlit
seabed.*

Making a seashore mask

To make your own disguise you will need a balloon, some newspaper, some shells and seaweed, half a cup of flour, and half a cup of water.

1 Mix the flour and water to make a runny paste and then blow up the balloon. Glue several layers of paper strips to the upper side of the balloon.

2 When the paper is hard and dry, lift the mask away from the balloon. If it is stuck, try popping the balloon instead!

3 Now cut out some eye-holes and add some shells and seaweed.

You can only see the underside of a ray's body when it swims.

Can you spot the sole that has buried itself in the seabed?

Breathing tube of a buried masked crab

Wear your mask to disguise yourself.

Underwater garden

What is the fastest-growing plant in the world? The answer is a seaweed that lives off the coast of California. Seaweeds have flat fronds instead of leaves. They are useful hiding places for small fish. See how many you can find here!

Brown seaweeds
Brown seaweeds grow at any depth. Wracks have narrow fronds. Kelps have broader fronds.

Wracks often live in tide pools.

Green seaweeds

Green seaweeds grow all over the shore and even in salty pools above the tideline. Unlike brown seaweeds, they are quite flimsy. If you take a green seaweed out of the water, it will turn into a soggy mess.

Wracks can be slippery underfoot – be careful if you walk on them!

Sugar kelp has fronds with crinkly edges.

Seaweeds may be covered with tiny animals.

Red seaweeds

All seaweeds need light to survive but red seaweeds can live in places where the light is quite dim. They often grow in deep water, but you can also find them in pools.

Sea lettuce often lives near fresh water.

Kelps have a special anchor called a holdfast.

Red seaweed

Holding on

If you can imagine being out in a hurricane, you will know what it is like for seashore animals when the waves crash around them. Waves are very powerful and seashore plants and animals can only survive them by holding on tight. If they let go, they may be hurled against the rocks and torn to pieces.

A hanging egg

Lesser spotted dogfish are small sharks that lay their eggs close to the shore. Each egg has a rubbery case and special tendrils that wrap around seaweed. The tendrils hold the egg safely in place while the young dogfish develops inside.

A dogfish egg can take more than nine months to hatch.

Sea urchins cling to the rock with hundreds of tiny sucker-tipped feet.

Stuck to a rock

Many rocky-shore animals use special suckers to keep them in place. This red blob is a sea anemone. It has fastened itself to a rock and pulled in its tentacles.

Getting a grip

Seaweeds do not have proper roots, but they are good at holding onto rocks. Sometimes a seaweed fastens itself to a rock that is too small and light. If this happens, waves may pick up both the rock and the seaweed and throw them onto the shore.

Sea anemone attached to hermit crab

Crab on the move

The hermit crab uses its strong legs to hang onto rocks. If the crab is threatened, it often pulls in its legs and drops into the safety of deeper water.

Starfish cling with tiny tube feet, just like sea urchins.

Hermit crab grips rock

Limpet covered with algae

Riding out the storm

A limpet has a large, suckerlike foot that can clamp its shell onto the rock. Even powerful waves cannot budge it.

Life adrift

How many living things do you think there are in a bucket of seawater? About a dozen? A hundred? A single bucket of seawater can contain millions of living things. Together they make up the "plankton" – a mass of life that drifts with the currents.

When they hatch, cod fry feed on plankton.

Fish fry
Cod release their eggs in the open sea and the eggs hatch into tiny "fry." Life is hard for these fish, and only a few survive.

Plants of the open sea
This strange object is a tiny plant. Its long "horns" help to keep it from sinking.

Deadly drifter
This tiny plant is far smaller than a pinhead, but it makes a deadly poison.

Plant in a case
Diatoms are tiny plants that float around in the sunlight. Each one is covered by a glasslike case.

Changing shape
When crabs are young, they often drift in the open sea. As they get older, they change shape and live on the seabed.

Mystery animal
This tiny animal is a baby sea urchin. Look on page 34 and you will notice it looks quite different when it grows up.

Paddling by
This young rock barnacle moves by flicking its tiny legs like paddles.

Trailing by

Like most seaweeds this kelp is fixed to something solid on the seabed, so it cannot move around. However, some seaweeds float on the surface of the sea. They drift with the currents and provide a home for tiny animals.

Long, feathery tentacles carry food to its mouth.

Floating fish

Jellyfish spend their lives drifting with the tides and currents. Once a jellyfish is on land, its body collapses and it cannot move at all.

Slow progress

A jellyfish moves by tightening and relaxing its bell-shaped body. When the bell tightens, it pushes water backward so that the jellyfish moves forward. Jellyfish cannot swim very fast and they often get washed up on beaches.

Making a meal

In the sea, food is often all around. Most of this food is made of tiny particles that are smaller than a pinhead. Some seashore animals spend all their adult lives filtering out a share of this floating feast. Others get their food by hunting or by bumping into it.

Tentacles armed with thousands of tiny poisonous stings

Danger adrift

The Portugese man-of-war drifts on the surface of the sea, and has long stinging tentacles that trail many yards into the water. If the tentacles touch a fish, they paralyze it and then pull it upward to be digested.

Tentacles curl up when they catch food.

A cuttlefish swims by rippling its fins or by shooting out a jet of water.

The living submarine

Cuttlefish are relatives of octopuses, and they catch their prey using tentacles. Inside its body, a cuttlefish has a special shell containing lots of tiny spaces. It can fill the spaces with fluid or gas so that it rises or sinks, just like a submarine.

Long hunting tentacles are surrounded by shorter arms to form a protective shield.

Eight-legged hunter

Octopuses hunt crabs and other small animals. An octopus will smother a crab with its long arms, and then give the crab a poisonous bite. Octopuses usually spend the day hidden in rocky crevices, and come out to feed only after dark.

An octopus can make its skin change color to match its background or to show what mood it is in.

Powerful suckers allow the octopus to grip and move quite quickly over the seabed.

An octopus swims by squirting a jet of water out of the base of its body.

Water flows in here

Water flows out here

Filtering food

A sea squirt is a tiny animal shaped like a bottle with two openings. It sucks in water and then filters out any particles of food that it contains. It then pumps the waste water out of the opening on its side.

Danger, keep clear!

When exploring the shore, remember that not everything likes to be touched or picked up. Most seashore animals are quite harmless, but some have sharp claws or even poisonous spines. A few have such powerful poisons that they can kill or injure people.

Warning signs

Animals that are brightly colored, like this lionfish, are often dangerous. The lionfish lives in the Pacific and Indian Oceans. Its stripes show that it has poisonous spines. The lionfish's poison is strong enough to kill a human.

Nasty nip

A green crab will nip you with its pincers if you accidentally step on it. It might hurt, but some shore animals are much more dangerous.

Deadly spines on fins

Deadly stone

The stonefish is a relative of the lionfish and it also lives in the tropics. It lies on the seabed and snatches any smaller fish that pass by. The stonefish has small spines that can inject a deadly poison. People sometimes die from stepping on it by accident.

Poisonous spines on fins

Coral attack

All corals catch their prey by using stinging threads. The fire coral's threads can pierce human skin and cause a lot of pain.

Danger in the sand

The weever is a small fish with poisonous spines. It is hard to spot as it partly buries itself in the sandy seabed.

The fire coral's bright yellow color warns that it is dangerous.

Shark in the shallows

The wobbegong is a shark that lives in shallow water around Australia. It lives on crabs and small fish, but it has been known to attack people who accidentally come too close.

Life in the dunes

When sand is dry, it is easily carried about by the wind. If the wind blows steadily from the sea to the land, it often pushes the sand into piles called sand dunes. Dunes have their own special wildlife. See the change as you walk inland from the sea.

Feeding by night

Snails that live on dunes feed mainly at night. During the day, they stay inside their shells to keep their bodies from drying out.

Feeding by day

You can often see sand lizards sunbathing before setting off to hunt. They get their energy from the warmth of the sun. The lizards then scuttle over the sand in search of small insects.

Changing landscape

The part of the dune nearest the sea is usually made of bare, shifting sand. Farther away from the sea, grasses begin to take root and hold the sand grains together.

Sea lyme grass is one of the few plants that can live on the seaward edge of dunes. Its stems creep beneath the sand.

Making sand move

In this project, you can see how the wind keeps sand grains on the move.

1 Put a block of wood next to an ice-cube tray. Now make a small "dune" by piling sand onto the block.

2 Make a wind blow sideways across the "dune" either by blowing through a straw or by holding a hairdryer close to the sand.

Hairdryer

3 The sand in the "dune" will be carried sideways by the wind. The heaviest grains will not travel far, but the lightest ones may reach the end of the tray.

Lighter grains may reach the end of the tray.

Sea bindweed grows on sandy beaches and dunes. It has fleshy leaves and seeds that float.

Damp hollows between dunes provide a home for animals such as this natterjack toad.

Marram grass is important to most dunes. It has long leaves that stop the sand moving about.

Sand couch-grass

The red-and-black cinnabar moth is often seen feeding from plants found on the dunes.

Sandy shore

Sand is soft to walk on and it is easy to dig up and play with. But have you ever wondered exactly what sand is, or how it is made? To find out about sand, you will need to give it a very close look.

Grains of sand are packed tightly together.

Glued by water

Sand castles are made from millions of grains of damp sand. When you build a sand castle, the water that surrounds each grain of sand works like glue and holds the sand castle together. If the sand dries out, the castle soon falls down.

Pores between grains are often filled with water.

Volcanic sand

This sand is made from the rock from a volcano. The sea grinds it down into a black sand.

Mineral sand

This forms when the sea grinds down rock that has formed in layers. It contains silica – the substance used to make glass.

Shell sand

This sand is made from tiny pieces of shell. Damp shell sand sticks to skin because most of it is flat.

Making a sand tray

You can start your own sand collection by making this special cardboard tray. Let the sand dry out before you add it to your collection.

1 Glue four large matchboxes together, side by side.

2 Carefully cut out rectangles of cardboard for labels. Fold them in half and glue them to one wall of each section.

3 Now pour your sand into each section of the display case.

Fine-grained sand made from gray layered rock

Coarse sand made of broken pieces of shell and coral

Fine-grained sand made from light-colored rock

Very coarse sand made from volcanic rock

Jumping to safety

If you walk along a sandy beach, you may notice clouds of tiny animals jumping out of your way. These are beach fleas – small relatives of shrimps and lobsters. They feed on rotting seaweed and jump by flicking their tails.

Coastal corals

Corals are small animals that often live close together. Many protect themselves by building hard cases. As the coral animals grow and then die, their cases pile up, and in some places they form huge banks called coral reefs.

If a large animal comes nearby, the polyps quickly pull in their tentacles.

Mushroom coral

Coming out to feed
These polyps (coral animals) are trailing their tentacles in the water to catch food. Their tentacles have tiny stinging threads that shoot out when a small animal brushes past them.

As cabbage corals grow and die, they help build coral reefs.

Mushroom coral
This coral contains just one polyp, protected by a stony cup that looks like the cap of a mushroom. It is not fixed to the seabed. If it is turned over, it can slowly pull itself the right way up.

Cabbage coral
This cabbage coral looks very much like a plant, but each of its "leaves" is made up of hundreds of tiny coral animals living close together. Cabbage corals live near the surface, where the water is sometimes rough.

Coral fans

Sea fans often grow in deep water and can be more than nine feet long. Instead of being hard and stiff, they can bend quite easily. Sea fans usually grow at right angles to the current. This gives them the best chance of catching any food that is drifting past. A large sea fan is often home to many other living things, including crabs, sponges, and barnacles.

This sea fan comes from the Fiji Islands in the Pacific Ocean. Its spreading shape shows that it is growing in calm water.

Gravel beach

Gravel beaches are made up of lots of small, rounded stones. They are quite difficult places for plants and animals to live since the sea keeps the stones moving. A lot of this wildlife lives high up on the shore, beyond the reach of the waves.

Searching for water
Gravel is full of air spaces and does not hold water. Plants that live on gravel need very long roots, so that they can reach the water far below the surface. They also need tough leaves, so they can cope with strong winds.

Sea campion grows in round clumps.

The beach pea is one of the few plants that can live on open gravel banks.

Sea holly has hard, prickly leaves.

Terns are small gulls.

Hidden on the beach

You might think that there is nowhere to hide on a gravel beach. But small birds like the ringed plover hide by looking just like stones. When the ringed plover moves, it is easy to see. But when it stops, it suddenly seems to vanish.

Disappearing eggs

Terns lay their eggs in hollows on a gravel bank. Their eggs have speckled patterns that make them very hard to see against the surrounding stones.

Tern's egg

A tern feeds by hovering above the water and then splashing down to catch small fish.

The ringed plover lays its eggs on muddy ground near gravel beaches. Its eggs are usually well camouflaged.

Oystercatchers are noisy birds with big beaks like chisels to pry open shells.

The yellow horned poppy grows seeds in a long pod.

Sanderling

The ringed plover feeds close to the water.

Water pipit

Rocky shore

For many plants and animals, a rocky shore makes an ideal place to live. Unlike gravel, solid rock does not get dragged about by the waves. Small plants and animals can live on the rocks without being battered to pieces or swept away.

Life from long ago
Rocky shores can be very good places for fossil-hunting. Fossils are the remains of plants or animals that have slowly turned to stone. This fossil is of an ammonite, which lived in shallow water. Ammonites were common more than 65 million years ago.

Layers of life
The best time to explore a rocky shore is at low tide. Some barnacles and periwinkles can survive out of water for a long time, so they can live high up on the rocks. Other sea animals, such as sea squirts and starfish, need to stay damp.

The ruddy turnstone scuttles over rocks, looking for small animals.

Lichens live on bare rock, just beyond the reach of waves. They grow very slowly, but live for a long time.

Bootlace worms can be over 15 feet long.

A beach flea will jump up if it is disturbed.

Sea squirts

Brittlestar

Most crabs hide at low tide.

Sucker-tipped feet

It's easy to recognize starfish because they are the only animals that have five arms. Underneath each arm are lots of small sucker-tipped feet arranged in rows. A starfish uses these to move and to open shells so that it can eat the animals inside.

Queen-Anne's-lace grows in dry ground on cliff tops. Garden carrots are close relatives of this plant.

Thrift grows on rocky ledges close to the sea. Its tough leaves are not harmed by salty spray from the waves.

Rock samphire has fleshy leaves that store water.

Sea anemones live close to the low-tide mark. They pull in their tentacles if the tide leaves them in the open air.

Periwinkles clamp themselves to the rock at low tide.

Tide pool

When the tide falls, most of the shore
is left high and dry. But in a tide pool, plants
and animals can stay safely underwater until
the sea returns. Every tide pool is different
– shallow pools sometimes have only a
few plants or animals, but deeper
ones may be packed with life.

High tide
At high tide, sea urchins
feed on tiny plants by
scraping rocks with
their powerful
teeth.

Low tide

At low tide, a tide pool still holds its water.
Seawater is usually quite cool, but in hot
weather, water trapped in a shallow tide pool
quickly warms up. Try putting your fingers in
a pool to test the temperature. If you look
around the edge of a shallow pool, you
will sometimes see tiny crystals of salt.
These are left behind when the
warm seawater evaporates.

*Anemones can
survive out of water
for a few hours.*

*Starfish have to find
damp places at low
tide. They creep
under rocks or
into tide pools.*

Muddy shore and marsh

You won't find people lazing on a muddy beach, or soaking up the sunshine in a seaside marsh. But for some plants and animals, muddy shores are perfect places to live. Although the mud is salty, it is also rich in nutrients and full of life.

Glasswort has fat, rounded stems and tiny leaves.

Glass from plants

Glasswort is a short, fleshy plant that lives close to the water's edge. Long ago, people collected glasswort and burned it because its ashes can be used to make glass.

Teal fly over marshes in the winter to look for food.

Marsh flowers

Like many saltmarsh plants, the sea aster flowers quite late in the summer. It grows away from the water's edge.

Sea aster

The painted lady butterfly feeds on the nectar from sea aster flowers.

Seaside terrapin

Most terrapins live in fresh water, but the American diamondback lives in salty water near the coast. It feeds at night and often spends the day basking in the sunshine.

Sea spurrey flowers close up quickly if the sun goes in.

Sea purslane has small yellow flowers. It lives at the inland edge of a saltmarsh, where the ground is drier.

Cord grass grows in wet, salty mud. It stops the mud from being washed away and helps turn it into dry land.

Lying in wait
A heron hunts by stealth. It wades into the water and then stands absolutely still. If a fish swims past, the heron stabs at it with its sharp beak.

Beauty in the marsh
Sea lavender has lots of small but brightly colored flowers, and in late summer it often turns whole marshes purple. The flowers keep their color if they are picked and allowed to dry out.

Sea plantain has narrow, leathery leaves and tiny flowers in long clusters.

Mangrove swamp

In warm parts of the world, muddy coasts are often covered by mangrove trees. Their spreading roots stop the mud from being washed away. A mangrove swamp is like a miniature jungle and it has its own special wildlife. There are animals living in the mud, on the roots, and clambering among the branches.

Living on leaves

Mangrove leaves are tough and leathery. For the proboscis monkey, they are an important source of food. These rare monkeys live in mangrove swamps on the island of Borneo. Male proboscis monkeys are twice as big as the females and they have very large noses.

Snakelike neck

Feathers dry in the sun.

Spread out to dry

Anhingas, or snakebirds, live in the swamps of the southern United States. They feed on fish and often swim with just their head and neck above the surface. After each fishing expedition, an anhinga spreads out its wings to dry.

Getting the message

At low tide the tiny fiddler crabs come out of their mud burrows to search for food. The male waves his outsize claw to attract a mate.

Stick in the mud

Mangroves are unusual trees, because they can grow in salty water. They have special roots which anchor them in the mud and breathing roots that collect air. A mangrove seed starts growing while it is still on the tree.

Mangrove seed

Home on a root

Many shore animals spend their adult lives fixed to something solid, such as a rock or a mangrove root. The roots soon become covered with mollusks and other small animals.

Fish out of water

Mudskippers are finger-sized fish that can breathe air. They use their stumpy fins to climb up mangrove roots. When danger threatens, they hop back into the water.

Mudskippers cling to root

Mangrove prop root anchored in the mud

Harbor and pier

A harbor is a busy place where boats are tied up and where fish are brought to the shore. Harbor walls are usually made of rock, concrete, or wood. Below the high-tide mark, tiny plants and animals settle here and soon it is full of life.

Fighting for food
Gulls are nature's scavengers. They eat almost anything, from crabs and dead fish to french fries and sandwiches.

Many harbors have rivers flowing into them. Their water is less salty than water in the open sea.

Keeping things clean
In busy harbors, the water can easily become polluted. This makes it difficult for sea animals to survive. If the water is clean, a harbor can be home to many different kinds of fish.

Top of the pile
Wooden pilings are
home to many small
animals and plants.
At low tide, some of
these are easy to see.

*A sea mat is a sheet of
tiny animals living
side by side.*

*Sea roaches hide
during the day.
At night they
look for food.*

Mussel

Sea anemone

Index

Cod fry

Fiddler crab

Underside of ray

R

S

Sea bindweed

T

WYZ

Gulls

Acknowledgments

Dorling Kindersley would like to thank:
Robin James and Mike Quarm from Weymouth Sealife Centre.
Tina Robinson and Susan St. Louis, Shakera Mangera and Mark Haygarth for design assistance.
Gemma Ching-A-Sue and Alison Owen for modeling.

Illustrations by:
Nick Hewetson, Tommy Swahn, Peter Visscher.

Picture credits
t=top, b=bottom, c=center, l=left, r=right.
David Burnie: 57r.
Peter Chadwick: 49t.
Bruce Coleman Ltd: 21cr, 23bl; Jen & Des Barlett 40t; / Jane Burton 37b; / Jack Dermid 54br; / Francisco Erize 23cr; / Allan Power 41b; / Fritz Prenzel 41t; / Dr Frederick Sauer 37c; / Konrad Worthe 21t.
Andy Crawford: 4cl, 4bl, 9b, 11t, 11b, 15c, 16, 17, 18-9, 20br, 22b, 24-5, 31cr, 44b, 48t.
Frank Greenaway: 4cl, 8tl, 9, 28, 29b, 30, 31cl, 31b, 323, 34, 35, 38b, 39, 40t, 41cr, 50t, 52-3.
David King: 8b, 37t.
Stephen Oliver: 44t.
Planet Earth: 46c; / Pete Atkinson 47; / Linda Pitkin 46t; / Rod Salm 46b.
Science Photo Library: 44c; / Dr Glen Feldman/NASA 12t.

Picture research: Diana Morris